The Arrows That Choose Us

The Arrows That Choose Us

Winner of the 2018 Press 53 Award for Poetry

Marilyn Annucci

Press 53
Winston-Salem

Press 53, LLC
PO Box 30314
Winston-Salem, NC 27130

First Edition

Winner of the 2018 Press 53 Award for Poetry

A Tom Lombardo Poetry Selection

Copyright © 2018 by Marilyn Annucci

All rights reserved, including the right of reproduction in whole or in part in any form except in the case of brief quotations embodied in critical articles or reviews. For permission, contact publisher at editor@Press53.com, or at the address above.

Cover design by Kevin Morgan Watson

Cover art, "Shore House, 1911," by William Bellows,
Public Domain

Author photo by Craig Schreiner

Library of Congress Control Number
2017964655

Printed on acid-free paper
ISBN 978-1-941209-75-2

for Jo-Anne Lazarus

The author wishes to thank the editors of the publications where these poems first appeared:

The American Poetry Journal: "Ghost Writer of Fortune Cookies" (published as "The [Failed] Ghost Copy Writer: Whole Foods")
Antiphon: "The Smallest Bones"
Arts & Letters: "Wrecked World" (also appeared in *Best of Poetry Daily*)
Chautauqua: "Archipelago"
Comstock Review: "Aubade"
Dogwood: "Cosmography" (won second place in the 2003 Tin House/Summer Literary Series, selected by Tom Sleigh)
HYBRID: "65 North"
The Journal: "In the Cathedral of Learning"
Southern Poetry Review: "The Crow"
Sou'wester: "Supplicants"
TAB: The Journal of Poetry and Poetics: "Iso·chron \n\:" and "Pre·mo·ni·tion \n\:"
Umbrella Journal: "By the Banks of the Daintree River"
Valparaiso Poetry Review: "Happened"
Verse Wisconsin: "Ghost Writer's Apprentice," "Ghost Writers' Nursing Home," and "Houdini Escapes the Time Capsule"
Wisconsin People & Ideas: "The Stray Dogs of Mexico" and "The Night of the Meteorite's Landing."

The following poems appear in the chapbook *Waiting Room*, winner of the 2012 Sunken Garden Poetry Prize, selected by Tony Hoagland (Hill-Stead Museum, 2012): "Remembering My Mother Sewing," "Supplicants," "The Crow," "Heart," "The Women of the Kazan Cathedral," and "The Stray Dogs of Mexico."

The following poems appear in the chapbook *Luck* (Parallel Press, 2000): "Remembering My Mother Sewing," "Questions of Purpose," and "In the Cathedral of Learning."

Note: "I have heard" is an erasure from page 116 of Virginia Woolf's *The Waves* (Harvest Edition, Harcourt Brace & Company, 1959), and "I will begin" is a very loose erasure from the same novel (primarily using words throughout pages).

Contents

Introduction — xi

I

Atrium — 3
Remembering My Mother Sewing — 4
The Smallest Bones — 6
Houdini Escapes the Time Capsule — 8
Mild Interrogation of Self as Vessel — 10
I was an ocean away — 12
Supplicants — 14
House of My Disillusions — 15
Ghost Writer as Genie — 16
Happened — 18
Questions of Purpose — 20
Ghost Writer of Fortune Cookies — 22
Wrecked World — 23
In Peter's City — 25
The Women of the Kazan Cathedral — 26

II

Heart — 29
pre·mo·ni·tion *n*\: — 30
I will begin — 31
Noli Me Tangere — 32
iso·chron *n*\: — 33
The Arrows That Choose Us — 34
I have heard — 35

III

She looked down — 39
Invention — 40
Three Musketeers — 41
Another Line — 43
The Ghost Writer of Westerns as Critic — 45
The Stray Dogs of Mexico — 46
Whole Foods — 47
Cosmography — 48
Ghost Writer's Apprentice — 50

Archipelago	51
Mid-Life Lookout	52
By the Banks of the Daintree River	53
After the Reading	54
Aubade	55
Ghost Writer's Ex-Wife	56
In the Cathedral of Learning	57
Cogito Ergo	58
The Annunciation	60
Descent	61
Deluge	63
This, Paradise	64
Lucky Enough	65
Ghost Writers' Nursing Home	67
The Night of the Meteorite's Landing	68
The Crow	69
65 North	71
Acknowledgments	73
Author Biography	75

Introduction
by Tom Lombardo, Poetry Series Editor

With pride and pleasure, I present to you the winner of the 2018 Press 53 Award for Poetry—*The Arrows That Choose Us* by Marilyn Annucci. In her debut collection, you will hear her ringing, original voice: East Coast attitude tempered by Midwestern reserve.

Intelligent and intense, her poetry is also simultaneously bleak and hopeful. Her poems move readers into a steady state of existence: Happiness is relative, but poem by poem Annucci builds a recipe to improve happiness in this strange and seemingly random experience we call living.

I hope you will be—as I was—captivated by her opening lines ("Atrium"): "The smallness in humans / cannot be measured, is too / big." And I hope you will stay captivated, as I did, until the collection's closing stanza: "I thought of the nameless the lonely the trapped...who might never get out" ("65 North").

When a poetry contest judge reads a submission through to the end, that's a very good omen. My question during my reading was this: "What is she doing that's drawing me through this submission?" Her stories are fresh and new, but, after reading over and over, I came to an understanding that Annucci's poetics are founded upon her startling, concrete diction that drives the vehicles and tenors in her use of metaphor, metonymy, synecdoche, all seasoned by a strong measure of irony and paradox. Between those opening and closing poems, I found poems filled with Annucci's imaginative figuration. Good poetry transports readers to places not normally examined in their own motives, loves, and fears, as they try to sidestep their way through life, and I found intriguing figures of speech and sound, poem after poem, drawing me through this collection to an understanding of the arrows that choose us.

In the title poem, those arrows "hover above us, pressing us / to live or love or be eaten by death." In "By the Banks of the Daintree River," Annucci figures one of the arrows as an Australian *Crocodilus* that might "jaw you / roll you down, drown you / without contest... / To be nothing / but fodder." Another of Annucci's arrows is a candy bar in "Three Musketeers" that causes a macabre death and an accidental shooting of two innocent connoisseurs. Later, the speaker in "The Ghost Writer of Westerns as Critic" aims an arrow of denial when he asks, "Who cares if no one knows I'm the shooter?" The arrows also pierce with desire or wisdom. For example, "Heart" refers to a past love affair, one in which the narrator has "fed the fatted calf of memory/ for years." And readers might encounter an epiphany in "Lucky Enough" as the narrator wonders "maybe everything has an unexpected use—/even the old griefs."

    I hope you enjoy *The Arrows That Choose Us* as much as I did, and that you will recommend this debut collection to your fellow poetry lovers. I'm proud to add Marilyn Annucci to the Press 53 canon of contemporary poets.

I

Atrium

The smallness in humans
cannot be measured, is too
big. After hurt or betrayal,

some wither. Others
close tight as the fist of a bud
and will not open again.

If they do, they do so
not in a wild forest
nor even an ordinary grassy yard

but in a safe, domed place
with others who lean toward the sun
which is far away through glass.

Remembering My Mother Sewing

I

Evenings I'd find you
        bent over the dining room table
                like a surgeon over a disembodied angel.

Under five yellow lights
        you would rearrange
                the wispy wings, pin them

to the floral cotton,
        the blue corduroy—
                the common material our bodies might fit.

This was the beginning
        of the reconstruction. You worked
                with a quiet determination,

the knuckles of your long fingers
        whitening
                as you applied the tiny teeth

of the tracing wheel
        against the delicate skin.
                Later,

after your careful unpinning,
        the anticipated sundering
                and airy uplift—

forgive me my moments of doubt—
        the mortal fabric
                would lie there, yes,

bearing the marks . . .

II

You knew in time
        the dress or slacks would grow
                too tight, or short,

that our days would be a succession
        of stepping in and out of pants and skirts,
                blouses and shirts,

of turning in the long mirrors,
        wanting beauty,
                lines that flatter,

cloth that carries the wearer
        when brains are not enough.
                Yet wanting more than that.

Despite the turtlenecks and scarves
        you wear today to hide
                your wrinkly neck.

One day it will all come off.
        Someone will bathe our bare bodies,
                maybe efficiently,

perhaps with revulsion or fear.
        If we're lucky
                with tenderness.

I cannot bear to think of you this way.
        Your lovely, bony body
                no more.

Your dress folded over a chair.

The Smallest Bones

1. Anvil

Under glass in the museum
you are small and white, a baby

tooth no fairy collects, and far
from the ear out of which you were

extracted. *Incus*, your Latin
name—the hard *k* hones

you, keeps your roots pointed
down, sharp as a fingernail

in a dark glove, in a dark
canal, vibrating.

2. Stirrup

The horses have gone off
without you, unsaddled, unbridled,

hooves like hollow mugs of wood.
If one could shrink and stand

beneath your tiny roman arch,
one might hear them, how they

echo across the cobbles, past
the high walls, as if the palace

were destination. The drum
distant and somewhere else.

And you, with your history,
your languages unrecoverable.

3. Hammer

You make audible the whisper,
the hush, whatever false phrases

linger behind fingers that eclipse
the mouth. What hesitates

to enter the coiled corridors
of the cochlea, arrives.

With a single fang you stare
down romantics who metamorphose

knives into flutes, boulders into songs.
What isn't heard clearly the first time

you repeat, you repeat, you repeat
until what has come through one ear

is nailed, cannot come out the other.

Houdini Escapes the Time Capsule

1.
It proved to be far deeper than a steamer trunk,
fraught with the stench and dirt of decades.
For the sake of nostalgia and to cop a cheap bath,
Houdini leaps from the Brooklyn Bridge in a Saks Fifth Avenue sack
only to be met by police, a gaggle of startled onlookers.
I am Harry Houdini.
Of course, you are.

America has changed utterly.
Internet, cell phones, advertisements beamed in neon
across Times Square he is nearly invisible
as he pulls yards of needles from his mouth at the corner
of 42nd Street only one woman stops.
I hope they're sterile.

What happened to the men in hats?
He misses especially the hats.

2.
And so he disappears to Wisconsin,
old childhood home,
Prince of the Air.

Houdini is on your porch, Houdini is
holding his breath in your bathtub.
It is not the Chinese water-torture trunk
but you are still impressed.

He is compact and muscular, passionate as he speaks
of humanity's illusions, rapt faces in the reflection
of ATM machines, masked sorrow in the lines at Walmart.
The need for escape even greater.

Not to be grumpy, he makes your cell phone ring when no one is calling.
Sometimes, he uses your computer to search Craigslist

for a straitjacket, unusual handcuffs.
There's a market, Houdini discovers, and not what he intended.

Houdini feels depressed.
Houdini misses Bess.

Yes, the washing machine is remarkable—
and the cake mixer fun to watch—
but mostly he wants to go back.

Where is the lock that opens the door to 1926
when that jerk of a boxer punched him in the stomach three times?
Houdini would stop him now, live out that slow and glorious stage

before the stock market crash, talkies, radio, Jews like himself
made into so many chattel, men shot apart, the sweat and nerves
of the deep South, the illusion of the shining kitchens of 1955.
He most likely would have died before Armstrong's *giant leap for mankind.*

On his way out—he does not say where to—
Houdini gathers a roomful of school boys,
sets up an ordinary computer screen,
counts to five.
See them disappear.

Houdini cannot bring anyone back.

Houdini is on a Boeing 787, taxiing down the runway;
Houdini is in the sky.

He orders a water;
he does not turn it into wine.
He is not Christ after all,
though Christ may be out there, too,

wringing his hands, uncuffed,
full of grief.

Mild Interrogation of Self as Vessel

Why did you not have a child?
Because I felt for years I was a child

Why did you not have a child?
Because it took my strength to live

Why did you not have a child?
Because I was
                afraid

Of?
Something growing inside of me

Did you ever want a child out of love?
Once. At times I thought—

                Mostly, I loved women

Not always?

But, surely, two women can have—

There were other things to do

                I feared I'd be impatient

And if you lacked patience, what could hap—?
I would become irritated.

I'm sorry.
But if you'd had a child out of love?
I would have loved that child to distraction.

Meaning you would have obsessed? Been too controlling?

May I go now?

Just tell me this: Under what circumstances might you have had a child?

Had I been a man I would have had a child.

Would you have been a good father?
Not nearly as good a father as I would have been a mother.

I was an ocean away

Nineteen and no e-mail, no Instant Message, no chat, no
nothing but a lumpy twin bed I sat on alone in gray and damp

England circa 1981, which means you might not have been
even a pixel in your mother's womb, not even one letter on a tiny screen,

and I was crying on a bed because I felt it   I felt what you do not
want to know   do not want to feel   do not want to

believe as you pick up your cell phone to say *Hey…*
I was a lone girl on a lumpy British bed in a priory with old nuns

who gardened and left me aerograms on the shelf below
the Holy Spirit stained glass window. And they were light blue, light

as the feathers of hope without wings. And down the streets the phone booths
were red, and it was glorious thrilling to find a broken one and call home

without stuffing the desperate ten pence down the silver throat.
It was getting away with something somewhere in a land not my own. It was

sweet crime on a three-speed bicycle down the road from bakeries warm
with loaves of bread. It was hearing the voices of my mother and my lover

and no way to reach them, no possibility   I was here   they were not.
Each of us alone as that gaunt self-portrait of El Greco in a dark chapel

at Oxford, that long face looking out at me, that somber organ music
afternoons I sat listening without Facebook, without wireless cafes—

those places nowhere in anyone's consciousness—as I sat thinking
El Greco might have painted his portrait in rain, in blue rain

and each of us was a vessel of desire and grief and nothing could change that,
nothing could block that out or swing our attention toward a big enough billboard

but God   who was   where was God?   those kids with Mohawks
and black boots breathing the gluey fumes and staggering outside Littlewoods

department store while young men in college sweaters punted on the Thames
and tutors talked of Mystery plays and a plowman's lunch and poets

buried in cathedrals, so when I returned to the priory I watched the nuns
work a small plot of soil outside the window where I sat beside a metal

pay phone and looked down, imagining sometimes jumping and how
the statue of the Virgin Mary could not stop me   No   each of us here for such

a brief time   no song in the background   no photograph of a friend
popping up to make me believe otherwise, to give me another screen.

This was the past and I was seeing clearly out the window at the trees
which were beautiful and distinct in their dark lines, in their rough skin,

and the sky was not virtual, did not exist as a black hole in someone's mind
but was straight-up air in which I was living the truth of my own

small existence, my own voice in my own head when I went out the door,
when I said goodbye   or did not   when I rode my bike through the walled

roads into the open street, down the hill, over the bridge toward Oxford.
I was the only one who knew where I was when I was passing the yellow

leaves, the stone gargoyles with their bugged eyes and thick tongues.
No GPS when I was pedaling the way blood pumps blood the way it does

when we are alive even if no one else knows we are   how we go on even when

                              no one can   reach us

Supplicants

    St. Petersburg, Russia

The saint behind the picture frame is aloof
and otherworldly as anyone behind glass.
Not much of a conversationalist.

Yet someone in a flowered kerchief
stops, rests her face against the pane.
Her lips move soundlessly, her shoulders

tremble, as if this were the Gate,
the one partition that keeps her
from Heaven itself. The saint's hand

lifts, but not to touch. Perhaps to bless.
He exists on the other side of these smoking
wicks, odor of stale coats, irreverent

clicks of cameras by curious tourists.
She doesn't mind. She brings her lips
to the glass, pauses long enough

to leave her breath. Draws back.
She wears simple shoes
and a plain, almost school-girl skirt.

And I want to know her
sadness, what she whispers
to the entombed one, her heart's desire.

When she leaves, an old man takes her
place, kisses near the smudge she left.
The human parts press against the holy.

House of My Disillusions

My last makeshift apartment appears in my dreams
as if I still live there. The sunny bedroom
with the green shades rolled crookedly on their cord,
the futon couch, the white ceramic sink
that broke my plates when I wasn't gentle enough,
and the old Underwood No. 5 typewriter
on the bare table in the otherwise empty study.

Pine crate with painted apples on the side.
Smell of smoke wafting up the air vents.
Squirrels tumbling down the walls from the attic,
and my landlord clanking in with cages to carry them off
to some far-away field. My landlord sitting heavily
at my kitchen table one day in the half light, drinking a beer,
surprised I was home early. He was going to paint, he said,
but in truth I didn't care. I needed places to go, too, sometimes,

away from Kim who lived behind me, her pink light
burning half the night, jazz always on, and her easy,
too easy, words once in bed: *tell me what you like in a lover*,
so I knew I couldn't trust her. Her step on my stairs.
Then there was the one who hooked her thumb
in my belt loop, hung on like that. Then didn't.
She'll always be married to her art, the visiting cartoonist told Kim
after meeting me at the feminist bookstore.
Her art will always come first.

I read about the cartoonist's death in the Bay Area years later.
The landlord's gone, too, a heart attack. I drive past the place
some days—it's not green anymore. It's somebody else's house
without squirrels between the floors. *Dreamer, wake up. You're not
even paying the rent.* Still, there's always a moment when the door
opens, and I look into the night air.

Ghost Writer as Genie

She rises out of the shower steam, the tea
pot, the fog that lifts over the struggling

writer's backyard, and presses her palms
against the panes. She sees the writer

sitting at the kitchen table, sniffling over
the story of his life, and she cries boo

hoo until he meets her eye, says *Okay,
you can do better?* She rearranges the air

and he's a boy again, playing snaps
in the school yard, playing beans,

working gimp, a gift for his mother,
who's never not sad, and he doesn't

want to cry and he won't, and the gimp
is bright yellow and orange, and braided

the way his mother braids her own hair
when she sits alone in the darkened bedroom

on the green chair and says I'm sorry when
he finds her bureau drawer laid out on her bed—

her scarves and Ponds face cream
and church missal and tears. She wants

to leave but has nowhere to go, she says.
He doesn't want that part of his story.

Take it out, he says.
So the ghost writer rubs the air

as if shining plates. And it's gone.
And the sadness on his chest lifts

like a spoonful of sugar, and the ghost
writer props her feet on the stove.

Dust of sun cones. She knows.
It's lonely behind words.

Happened

When my brother asks if I heard
what happened to his old friend,
and says "terrible" and "sad,"
in the moments of my still

unknowing I see him, Paul, as a boy
in a blue striped shirt sitting on our porch
talking and laughing, or playing
tag and hide 'n seek, and only later

did I learn that he was good in math
and realized he was wry
and was surprised
to hear he fell in love and married

and there was steady work and
parties. A certain happiness.
And then divorce,
a shock, and Paul came back

to where his father lived alone
on the street we all had fled,
and I thought of that gray house
as if his mother were still there

how she would drink most days
and tap on the back window
when we played, her dark hair
piled high on her head.

Their kitchen table was wood
with benches, like a booth
at Friendly's, and there were times
his mother talked to us, her voice

breathy from Winstons, the smoke rising
like a halo that never stayed,
though Sundays she walked down
the center aisle of our church,

her black veil shrouding her face,
all the way to the front row
closest to the priest, where she knelt
with a stillness and contrition.

And Paul's pale Irish father
used to blink and blink
when he said hi, as if everything
moved too quickly, and it did.

Questions of Purpose

The woman I live with, meaning my partner (but
not business), my friend (but more than that),
my lover (but only sometimes), my significant
other, wife-but-not-really is crying tonight
while I sit on the other side of her wall
working words that will tell you, stranger,
I am sick of her heaviness, of her sobbing.
Words that sound selfish and cold.

My friend Martha Looney used to sing
Make the world go away
Get it all off my shoulders
in the asphalt school yard
when we were 13 and knew already
how sadness was big as the world, which meant
big as our families—
my own mother glum at the kitchen table,
my father angry about the Puerto Ricans and long-haired men,
whatever he let keep him from his own grief.
Martha would sing the words in a pitch so
desperate, so urgent
we could only laugh at our helplessness,
at our own small lives, waiting for the bell to ring.

My significant et cetera needs to know
why she's here, meaning in the world,
what it is we're meant to do—
questions of purpose that haunt me, too,
though I like to think I'm here partly to comfort,
which means I'm sad when I cannot,
when I'm too sick of sorrow myself, too tired
of tears, like tonight, tired even of language
which will never let me tell it all, never get this right,
how sometimes I miss Martha Looney, her sad funny song,

miss, too, the times I'd chase her down the street with dog doo
on a stick until she'd stop, swing
toward me like a lunatic, eyes rolling
so that I'd drop the stick and scream, so that we'd break
into wild laughter, bent double in the street,
and it would be enough.

Ghost Writer of Fortune Cookies

The fortune cookie, like the clam,
keeps its own counsel. Who made

the mollusk? Who wrote the proverb?—
neither matters, only that

The circle is running in the right direction.
When the shell lies empty

as a shallow bowl, do not toss it
without thought. *Do not put cold manners*

on show. Rather lift it to your ear
and hear the sea rush that washed it

to your shore. When the cookie
lies cracked, raise it to your tongue

and taste the plain vessel that carried
such glad news: *Your life will soon be*

graced with happiness. Stay today.
Lucky numbers 11 5 22 19.

Wrecked World

Your dishpan quiet as a pond,
all the white ambition
shrunk to mild foam. You

have been away too long,
cups and plates tilt like glaciers.
Man: the toppler of worlds.

You wedge your hand
between what shifts
and slides, methodically

descend, layer by cool
layer, until your fingers crawl
along the smooth bottom,

amphibian.
This is where the knives lie,
mute battleships gone down

on their sides. How wonderful
to find them unaware
and then to pull one, nose

up, and up
until it hangs in the stunned air —
wrecker in a wrecked world.

Were you wrong to dredge it up? —
Is there not meat to cut, and pie?
Wrong to pour warm water

down the long length of its side,
to place it in the company of spoons,
which seem so soft, yet do not lie;

when you hold the knife
before one oblong eye —
concave or convex,

right-side up or upside down —
you see how the blade stretches
from your head to heart,

so much bigger than you thought.

In Peter's City

"It is not that this is a bad conversation," she said,
"but it is not necessary." And so I surrendered,

if only for moments, my American small talk,
sat quietly at a table reddened by wine and pickled cabbage

with this woman whose pink shirt hugged her breasts.
Who was she to have said my skin was fair,

to have let her eyes rest on the curve of my shoulder.
Native for nearly half a century of this northern city,

friend of an acquaintance, she wished to make me,
in three days' time, mushroom soup—"it is not easy

to find poisoned ones," she assured me. In the room
adjoining a man sang Russian love songs—

her eyes grew wistful, grew daring:
"It has been a long time since I danced.

And you?" Only later did I think of the sphinxes
over the Neva, the riddles in their stone.

"It has been a while," I said. And yes, the room was wide
enough, and maybe because it was so, I turned

our talk somehow to Pushkin, who was given an invitation
to die, and did not resist. In this city marked by famine,

by wars, why couldn't I have lifted her to the floor, why couldn't I
have admitted she was beautiful—and still have lived?

The Women of the Kazan Cathedral

    St. Petersburg, Russia

Quick ancients in kerchiefs
move quietly as breath

among carousels of candles,
snuffing the slender tapers

like stumps of cigarillos,
tossing them into the tin pail.

If the inch of wax still holds prayer,
still possesses the pilgrim's desire

to burn all the way down,
It doesn't matter

these Mothers of Christ
say with their silence,

say with their refusal
to meet your eyes.

Another stub, another prayer
has burned long enough.

II

Heart

A friend tells me your heart is giving out.
Not the way it gave to me when rumors
swished and gasped—

a heart-shaped kiss on a flush cock—
but giving out like a possum on a hot road.
The helpless human heart

in need of someone to traffic the blood,
to bring the miracle of tiny balloons
and let you walk away. The foot

you claimed to be half in the grave
is now my own. I can finally say
I know what you mean

how the years can feel too big
to build again—the love you have
becomes the love that has you, too.

Your son, the wife who is your friend
after all. Call it settling.
Call it deepening

I still don't know for sure.
I certainly didn't know then.
I'm embarrassed to say

I've fed the fatted calf of memory
for years—the conversations
we continue, the sex I rewind:

Strange alchemy of the past: no ashes
but the marsh of fire. No fire
but the lungs and hands and heart.

pre·mo·ni·tion \ *n* \:

1. [to warn in advance] Something in the grass in the stones
between the brick campus buildings / in the slope of the hill /
the way he lugged / that canvas bag of books / too full /
his hair thick   his glance / an uncommon attention / 2. [to know
the inevitable]: inside an office / the blue in his shirt / he made her
laugh / and when he spoke / in the classroom / Steinbeck's
"Chrysanthemums" / by then it was too late / *Elisa poured herself /
into the flowers / the blooms as big / as her hands* / He opened
his own hands / they kept opening / the chrysanthemums
were enormous / red   they must have been / red / he understood /
she wanted so much / more than

I will begin

        And if I begin—

No   another day

Some animal pushes

      through the unopened flowers

      the body

            is stronger than

Let us say

            we became unrecognizable

scent   no   single

                face

relics of myself

           and this undressing

   like a field bearing heat

Noli Me Tangere

    After the painting by Francesco de Mura

Noli Me Tangere, Jesus says
to Mary Magdalene
when she recognizes him
after his resurrection.
He doesn't want her

to touch him, doesn't want her
to cling to him
for he has not yet ascended.
He holds out his beautiful arm
in a gesture that says Stop.

But why?! Magdalene seems to be asking
as she reaches toward him.
This is not at all the priestly Jesus
on the Road to Emmaus, his eyes heavenward
as he breaks bread with the disciples,

but a newly voluptuous Jesus,
his halo a golden haze,
his lips rosy,
his chest muscular.

Having planted our eternal seeds,
he's carrying a hoe
and on his way to heaven.
But why go?
everything pleads

even the languorous cherubs
who lean together like lovers on a creamy cloud.
The sky is a deep turquoise,
Magdalene's robe a blood red.
What could be greater

than this? The sumptuous
body.
Stay.
Don't save us.
Save us.

iso·chron \ *n* \ :

I was   vacuuming and you were

dying somewhere

east in the world of   maps and miles

which is   not

the sphere of grief   or love

because   you found me   and I

turned

from the dust / from the walls / from the stairs /

and collapsed

                          sobbing

on a Friday afternoon

How did I know

I could have disappeared

like a bead

in the carpet   like hardened

mud from a boot

had I not turned off the switch

had I not turned from

the terrible roar   of your leaving

The Arrows That Choose Us

The ones who hover above us, pressing us

to live or love or be eaten by death

are smaller than ferns, taller than goats,

redder than blood, cold as snow inside snow

inside caves of rock or shadows or

a garden's hell. They exist in mud, in a sky

beyond sky, in a mind that won't stop,

in the white light where duty calls,

where tunnels are wrought,

where strange creatures move forward

bearing black bones, talons, words, the prick

of desire, whatever is needed to tear us awake.

I have heard

  my   obliterating

                       tide

                this drumming

                           of enormous

            happiness.

        I could say

                              Heaven

                                          The hour is still

III

She looked down

        the lamp-strung fields
          of death

                                        Yes, she realized that

Invention

Stumbling into the kitchen at 2 a.m., I grope for the light,
think of Thomas Alva Edison who brought this easy

incandescence into our rooms. While the world slept,
he took only cat naps—on the floor, a desk, a pile

of coal. While men snored or lay tense with dread,
he searched for the loyal filament—coconut hair,

fishing thread, bamboo. And from such delicate lines
grew sockets and switches, workmen and wires,

fourteen miles of trenches beneath a city square.
Above one leaky main, horses danced sparks

on the electric sidewalk. Through frozen winter
into talk of spring. Evening all aglow.

So who hasn't tossed in the tight-mouthed
dark and wondered: What has *my* sleeplessness brought?

Three Musketeers

Something silver floats in the ocean
like a slip of gutted fish.
Then you see the red
lettering, and the thin white and blue
Thre—a tear where the second
e should be—*Musketeers*.

Imagine America, 1932,
the year of the chocolate bar's invention,
the year unemployment reached 13.7 million
and breadlines and soup kitchens
sprawled across the country.
. . .and one for all!
A time for heroes on horses.

But in the end we have only the confection,
the sweet aftertaste.
Not the French musketeers,
or King Louis XIII or XIV
or even a drifter named Daniel
who spent three days in Indian River County jail
for stealing a Three Musketeers from a 7-Eleven,
and later froze to death from exposure
in Sea World's whale pool.

And we have, temporarily as we have ourselves,
Andre Burgess, who, in 1997,
while enjoying this fluffy chocolate
treat and walking down the street,
this black, high school soccer star
was shot in the leg by a cop who thought
the silver wrapper was a semi-automatic pistol.

We have the lethal wrapper.

And, of course, we have the sea—
not the chocolate lover who once stood there,
hungry in the salty foam.
Was he old? Was he young? Was he *she?*—
We have the sea,
which undulates and syncopates,
pulls and churns, yawns and dawns,
rises and recedes and breaks—
but *never* flushes—
over and astonishingly over
the sea buckling with dying algae and sick fish
with spilled oil, downed planes and broken ships
with whatever we've dropped and keep dropping:
cigarette butts, bombs, plastic bottles, bungees, Schlitz.

And the Three Musketeers wrapper
coming in on the tide.

Another Line

> *Though I fail, I weep:*
> *Though I halt in pace,*
>   *Yet I creep*
> *To the throne of grace.*
>   —George Herbert

1.

This is for cousin Darren
killed in Queens

      Not for the car
hard-braking beside him—

the gun at point blank.

      Not for the glass that broke
across Darren's girl

her screams
gold leather seats.

      Not for the bullet
sunk in Darren's heart.

Darren

twice stopped.

2.

But for the neighbors who tried to help

who opened thin doors
carried tired selves down cement steps

into the ordinary street.

3.

For the skin we're stuck in
the blood that won't stay in.

And the money, which continues to matter.

4.

This is for Darren's heart,
not the one stilled by a bullet

but the whole heart, the boy in the back
of my parents' brown station wagon

the curly-haired cousin from New York
who pressed his finger to the foggy glass

so many years ago, and wrote—
smirking shyly between my brother and me—

Darren + Marilyn
knowing this was just a little bit wrong.

This is for that boy, for all boys
undamaged yet.

The Ghost Writer of Westerns as Critic

> LITTLE BILL: I don't... deserve this... to die this way. I was... building a house.
> MUNNY (aiming his pistol point blank): "Deserve" don't mean shit, Little Bill.
> –David Webb Peoples, *Unforgiven*

Can't stop thinking of Peoples' *Unforgiven*, how
Hackman sat on it. Took years for Eastwood to see it,

make it that good. Munny's right about
"deserving" adding up to nothing in life's equation.

If he weren't, I'da had a horseload of scripts
by now. Ain't no one works harder. I'm old-

fashioned, too, changing my own typewriter
ribbon, whiting out errors like bleaching blood

from a dead sonofabitch's shirt, them keys
below my fingers banging like bullets in a bar.

Who cares if no one knows I'm the shooter? Little
Bill's mistake wasn't drawing his revolver too slow,

but thinking he'd made a home, s'if a sheriff could
stake down roots in some cow town with drunken

gunslingers and 'spect to die natural. Must have taken
a miner's piss to make Bill that jackass funny—

and mean as fire in a mare's mane. Don't know why
Munny didn't ride off with Delilah. Beautiful

and scarred, she'd of left whoring, kept him
clean from whiskey and killing. 'Course he had

them children needin' a mother. Moonlighting
romances is making me soft. Never expected as much,

riding into a sunset that weren't an open wound.

The Stray Dogs of Mexico

One crosses the street, ribs
like ladder rungs leaning

inside him. I want to climb
to God, ask and ask.

The streets are full
of crushed plastic bottles.

The mountain air has left us
winded. On the coast

we sit in open huts, wear
flip flops to the shore,

each grain of sand a small fire
dogs run across. Desperate

with thirst, one sips from the sea.
They are the poorest of poor,

tails down, unable even
to pour themselves water.

"We're all stray dogs," someone says.
But we're not.

I fill a small cup, set it before one
who drinks without stopping.

Whole Foods

are so much better than little bits, little chewed off
pieces of foods one might leave for a bird or a woman
without a home. Not whole, as in lacking parts: broccoli
without heads, potatoes missing eyes. Maimed foods.
Pork chops on their last legs. Tomatoes with their skins
blown off. Bread crumbs. The whole crumby world out
there, not in here. Whole, as in what more could you ask
for: bright organic peppers in the jet of the spritzer. Crisp
stalks of celery, fennel, white asparagus. Complete, as in
all of us together, smiling, restored, fully realized as we reach
for that tiramisu. Rich, as in not poor, not stuck with radiated
beef, milk, mutated chickens, as in not free, not free-range at all.

Cosmography

When I look closely at my countenance, I am afraid
I see an early alphabet ghosting
beneath this modern text. Something

like a splotch of ɑ claims me, among other mysteries.
After all, this skin is not unlike a fifteenth century leaf
in need of preservation. Consider the neglected

volumes in a seminary somewhere near Seattle
that a Jesuit brought back from Florence in the 1960s—
late medieval missals perfumed with must,

vellum pages and gothic miniscule to bend the reader
earthward as he pondered the weight of visions.
When scholars came, not one could spare the time

to catalog or to preserve, and decades passed
and few remained who even read the letters Þ
 and ð, morphed to dust on curious fingers,

recalling the Lenten ritual *and unto dust*
thou shalt return, like a thumb
of newsprint on an aging Jesuit's brow.

And now it is he who is the last to know these books,
and so his task remains: to call these remote words
into a kind of order, to preserve for a few decades more

their place, as I might try to preserve my thinning
skin, or, you, this poem on paper, acid-free
or, better yet, in endless space that swims into a screen

and goes where rockets do not even go, infinity
of sorts, the kind scribes never dreamed.
Who could have guessed that text would surface

from such empty air and not grow cold? Or not grow
old, as bodies surely do. Celestial,
each word might seem, a luminary mask—

it hardly matters that the face is gone.

Ghost Writer's Apprentice

He's assigned the most invisible
jobs: *Ramp Closed* or *Milwaukee*

Right Lane. It takes its toll
after the one hundredth mile marker,

and he starts to speculate about
the blur of passengers and mufflers

and songs he can't hear
through closed windows. Alive,

he never gave them a thought.
Never wondered who wrote *Rest Area*

or the numbers and names
of exits on highway tickets he handed

to booth operators, then sped off.
He would have said bureaucrats,

if pressed, but no one asked.
Sometimes he conjures the small print

on leases, death certificates, estate
sales. Before he can inhabit

the spaces of others, he must
experience humility, an absence

of ego. *Yield.* And he has begun to—
a white line down a divided highway.

Not solid, but broken. Passing
into anonymity, and back.

Archipelago

When Mrs. Sayres came for dinner, she was thrilled with my mother's good cooking, and sat like a captain in her square shoes and dresses that blossomed with roses at the head of the dining room table. She had married a doctor who had passed on, and now she traveled, mostly on ships. She enchanted us with tales of villages and dark whisperings, treasures and wild elephants, as if she were a living View-Master of the world. Artifacts filled her large home, whose windows my father washed, whose rooms my mother cleaned. Once she entrusted my parents with a Chinese garden urn for safekeeping. My mother kept it upstairs, dusting it and watching over it as if the bedroom were a vault. We were guarding something burglars would break down doors to steal—only three in the world, my mother said. It was cool to the touch, glossy and sophisticated with its watery lapis birds. Its mysterious air. Big enough to hold a child. Or some quiet grief.

In her old age, Mrs. Sayres' memory grew scattered. She wandered down streets or got into the gin. Faithful, my mother washed her soft arms, neatened the small rooms her daughters had arranged. Finally, even that was too much, and she was moved to a nursing home she claimed was a ship. She spoke of her state room. How lovely the cruise. She seemed not to know her daughters had left her. Only that she floated on some unnamed sea.

Mid-Life Lookout

Thin as a sock puppet
my neck rises
to offer you my head
Hello out there.

Sometimes my friend eyes
the skeleton that lives
inside me, "Eat!"
Still, my neck stays
lean—swallowing,
swallowing.

It grows old ahead of me.
It holds the talking head of me.
Pivots

east, west,
north, south—
a lighthouse
on a black night:

mercy

                mercy

By the Banks of the Daintree River

   North Queensland, Australia

Crocodilus, as in
it might sense your shadow, or, worse,
the flesh of you. It might
pull the enormous stone of itself
out of the brown waters
into the flash of air; jaw you,
roll you down, drown you
without contest.

You, who never thought
you would "go out" this way,
to be snouted deep into a river's
rocks and branches and silty leafage,
fed on for days.
To be nothing

but fodder, you, who believed in science,
progress, your body
below the sterilized implements of medical students;
you who signed the donor card,
imagining your heart somewhere
still beating; even you
who wished to be tucked in the earth
like a root vegetable, to leave
seepage and grass.

Not these bones—
monkey? fawn? boy?—

clanking together like rocks in the shaker of tide.
Who would have guessed
they would give you up so easily—
your loves, your questions,
even your most delicate stance,
like a pied stilt in low water.

After the Reading

People said nice things and smiled
and gathered their bags and umbrellas—
those who had anticipated—as it had
begun to rain and was getting dark,
and I could tell that a few were feeling
uneasy because they were no longer young,
were getting old, in fact, like their
parents, who had left them, and now
someone's daughter had cancer,
and another had lost two brothers,
and it took only a moment to look
out the window toward the dark
street with lights from a few cars—
their eyesight wasn't what it
used to be—to wonder who would
or would not care for them one day,
and where they would go.

It would have made perfect
sense, really, to lie down
right there on the polished floor
with the rugs, or to curl up
in the doorway, wet now
from the rain, and let ourselves—
any one of us—just be
exhausted, maybe even loved,
touched on the head by strangers
or stroked like a dog, simply
to be how we were when we
discovered ourselves for the first
time in this world, no language
but a long wailing.

Of course, we were in a bookstore,
and it was night, and we needed
to take ourselves home.

Aubade

We leave in the hour
of film noir. Neighbors'

eaves and porches,
trash cans, shady

shapes, your suitcase
lifted into our car's

back seat. Traffic lights
blink yellow all the way

down Johnson Street,
and the sky begins

its slow resolution,
whitening. Your hand

closes in mine. You'll be
onboard soon, matter

of fact, will settle in
to your seat, call me

from your cell, take out
your book, gaze out

the window as the plane
noses into the clouds

and you look down
one last time—roads,

farm fields, loves.
Freighted into all this light.

Ghost Writer's Ex-Wife

He remembered Greta Garbo's birthday—
September 18, a Virgo, of course—

but not mine. Garbo didn't need
Talkies with that face, he would say,

though he couldn't imagine *Camille*
without her. He adored stuffing

words into beautiful women's mouths.
Well, I've got my own mouthful now,

back from the dead, Daddy's old
apparition. I braised asparagus,

roasted duck—while he sat at a table
laid by invisible hands. His eyes,

all aperture, closed on air:
"Only Germany appreciated Louise

Brooks, you know." He tried to write
to her years after *Pandora's Box*.

"Cursed Hollywood," he would say,
"shallow as an A-cup." He liked

brothel scenes—tawdry couture,
sassy lines. But I was the real

vision, the wife in the light
of the TV box—there, not there.

In the Cathedral of Learning, Pittsburgh, 1997

> *There is so much Everything*
> *that Nothing is hidden quite nicely.*
>   —Wisława Szymborska, "Reality Demands"

Words get lost in the vaulted air.
Light gets lost;
there is no pink, yet
there is this pink glow.
Wrought iron, round
wooden tables—
a quiet veranda, or a street;
all the horses have disappeared.
A man's voice rings out,
processing . . . computer . . .
It is, of course, the end
of the 20th century; other voices
flutter at the muffled edges:
bats, moths.
A woman coughs;
there is something she cannot say.
Bing.
The elevator door slams shut—
not like a boxcar,
not like a row of grocery carts.
A man's heels click
on the cold floor.
Does anyone hide in the oak bench?
It lifts like an old school desk.
Down the darkened halls,
along the heavy doors,
invisible robes
touch the floor like prayers.
No one sits in the alcove
with stained red glass.
Stone ivy, iron daffodils.
The light over the tables glows white;
my hands, a friend said, look old.
I cannot pretend I will last as long
as the fluted arches, or the steel grids.
Look, how they make the space above
safe enough to lean toward.

Cogito Ergo

I thought the apple
was its rosiness
until my lips
my teeth my tongue
opened

I knew the apple then
was this
astonishment
of tart
and sweet

I met
with all my hunger
all my breath
and yet
it was not this

but something
dark it spilled to me
I knew the apple
deeply then
how it had grown

but I was wrong
again
the apple
was no more than snow
as cool as what I thought

I'd known
forgotten out of grief
until this spring
this swoon
of strange perfume

of apple
everywhere and nowhere
yet
so much
this nothing that I knew

The Annunciation

> After the painting by Francesco de Mura

Everything's soft and billowy,
the clouds engulfing Mary
like Styrofoam balls

in the holy box
in which Gabriel finds her, turning
as if for a moment

from her gold reading desk
over which she seems
to have been kneeling,

alone with her bible
and now Gabriel,
his two large wings erect,

his one arm raised
to heaven, a luminous cloth
falling from his bare shoulder

as if he carries the sun
and a lily in his other hand,
which she will accept, too.

Descent

The Irish pub was cave-like with candles
on the dark pine tables and soft yellow

lights along the walls, so maybe
talk of the British tin mines wasn't so unusual

when the Irish musicians took a break
and the crowd stopped snapping photos

and showing one another their pictures
as if to prove we were really there.

In the mines, a donkey was really there,
according to one of the British men

who sat down with four friends at our table
and told how the animal was lowered

and forced to stay in that dusty, hot, airlessness
until it got sick. Someone ordered

a pint, and laughter burst from another table.
When a doctor told the miners the donkey

needed grass, they finally hauled it up,
and the animal wouldn't go back down.

Kids were sent into tin mines, too,
the man's friend added. Younger ones,

and women worked from dawn to night
breaking up the ore above ground.

We were above ground, and on holiday
as one of the men put it. Just that morning

I had gone to a perfumery
that made fragrances from wildflowers

that managed to grow in the fissured
limestone. Beautiful bursts of scent

rose from tiny vials, tall glass bottles,
bright bars of soaps.

I hadn't heard about donkeys in tin mines
but donkeys and mules had spent

entire lives in the darkness of coal mines,
hauling the heavy wagons.

Pit ponies in Britain were even
stabled underground, one man added.

Someone said chimney sweepers,
children—wasn't that equally horrible?

It was. They were. Then mercifully,
the musicians returned, bearing all

the mournful ballads. And the crowd
lifted its cameras again.

Deluge

When the rain comes
like gossamer
steel and taps and
taps the pavement
and seeps
beneath the doors
and pushes
through windows
and fills rooms
like the tide inside a snail
so that even the credenza
dislodges
and rises
like the moment in a séance
when the wingback chairs
sit closer to the ceiling than to the floor

even the hat boxes
stowed for decades
with the dresses
in the closet
spill their ovals of mauve straw
float like lifeboats
garlanded with African violets
and poppies
and something that looks like a ribbon of eel
that leaves by the bedroom window

This, Paradise

The young waitress calls Palm Cove "a paralyzed paradise,"
    then tries to make that sound like a good thing—
        "away from everything, you know," but I feel her
            unrest, her longing for cities, lovers, live bands,

not these nocturnal tropical birds that scream
    outside our balcony at midnight, cluck-barking
        into the black air, not these chilly days—a cold wave
            off Antarctica, and all the boats to the Barrier Reef

docked, waiting for the waters to calm. Yet we want
    nothing else, halfway across the world on a beach
        that warns swimmers of box jellyfish (the grisly
            museum exhibit is evidence), in restaurants

that serve Barramundi and grilled steaks, red
    cabbage diced with red grapes. It hardly matters
        that salties rise from the river to feed on human legs
            and the heads and bodies of guileless cows. Or that

I don't know what my lover thinks, nor does she
    of me as we sit reading. John Bayley writes of his life
        with Iris: *Such ignorance, such solitude!—they suddenly*
            seemed the best part of love and marriage. And yes,

it *is* paradise, this night when we suddenly clasp
    one another's hands, two old girls, and race down
        the cobbled streets, laughing, to our apartment,
            to what feels like our very own, the way we fling

open the shutters and lean toward the palm fronds
    to hear this new bird call, so strange, like a thin
        whistle above the creek water, which runs all night,
            the way it rains sometimes, and keeps on raining.

Lucky Enough

This is the summer
I'm learning the names of flowers.
When I bow to the little pink and white ones—
the fringed pinwheels—
I can now say *dianthus*,
though sometimes I slip, say *delphinium*.
Hello delphinium.

And I've names for the lovely frivolity,
the bright orange crepe,
the pretty girl's party skirt,
the one we call *poppy*.

How is it I'd never even *thought* to plant peonies—
those blousy pink wonders
from whose plush petals
I expect a tiny heiress to rise
stretching and yawning.

These mornings I often sleep until 10:00.
It's uncommonly cold and I like to lie dreaming.
The flowers, too, are in their beds;
though sometimes I think, *they're* up,
they've been living their flower lives
in the chilly air of dawn.
What have you done?

It's taken me many years
to know even the littlest things—

that this is a pansy, for instance,
this yellow clover butterfly flying only on a stem.
And just last month I learned *petunia*;
not that I'd never heard the name,
but now it's *petunia*,
trumpeting from every window
box and planter
I see on my walks.

It's easy not to notice almost everything in life.
I catch myself tallying, taking stock,

and I feel things slipping
through my fingers,
like the cocoa beans
my friend spread as ground cover.
They smell sweet
and have this unexpected use.
I tell myself
maybe everything has an unexpected use—
even the old griefs,
the *almost* birds in hand.

Or maybe it's like the moonflower,
which blooms only after sundown
and closes by noon next day—
a delirious bloom,
midsummer to first frost,
and that's its life.
It does what it does,
and whoever was lucky enough to have been there
was lucky enough.

Ghost Writers' Nursing Home

No one talks about their *own* lives.
And the stories of movie stars,
presidents, and divas

are old. It's nice to sit,
let someone else *dish*—
well, it's worth a snicker

over lunch among goblin gossips
out to pasture. Rarely
do they feel regret. The *coulda*

been a contenda crap. Someone
shuts them up. Big name:
steam on a mirror. Done.

Out back there's birds and a feeder,
and enough stories to last a—
Don't need those either.

The Night of the Meteorite's Landing

It basically got light as day here.
And it rumbled like a trolley car.
    —Bob Dowr, bartender, Alley Oops Tavern, Livingston, WI, April 14, 2010

I must have been in the underground
garage at the time, thinking

my meter had run out, hoping
I wouldn't get a parking ticket,

then relieved when my windshield
was bare. Icarus could have fallen

into Lake Mendota for all the dumb
ox I was, plowing my way home

up University Ave., left onto
Franklin. I don't even remember

stars above trees. I barely
remember trees. And I was sober

as a pad of paper, while the guys
down at Alley Oops dropped

their beers and squinted out
into a night blasting with light—

God's trolley car sparking
on the tracks to take them

heavenward. And then not.
But they had a story to tell.

I pulled into my dark driveway,
hurried up the front walk.

A bright light blinked on,
the way it does.

The Crow

He could have been an executive, a despot,
one of our president's own men. Impatient
in the backyard, he paced furiously,
eyeing the trees, the sky, waiting for bishops,

linguists, kings. He fidgeted at the fence,
hurried across the grass, turning south
then west. Irritation in his gait.
He hated slang, that pidgin Crow,

the lazy calls and whiny cawing. His wife
had left him. Fool, cuckold, failure.
And now he dragged one broken wing
that frayed like loose-leaf paper.

To hell with them—numbers, sycophants,
continents. He should have left her,
and now when he beat his wings
to rise he couldn't even reach the sill.

Humiliating, the way the sky never moved
and those trees and that glossy creature
in the high branches so much like himself
only not, not anymore, how he squawked.

Rabbits scampered among the arborvitae.
He could have picked their soft fur to pieces
near as noon. What was he to do, what
was he to do? He hadn't realized how

disappointing ground could be, how
limiting, really, especially with these posts
he could neither fit through nor scale, though
he tried, penned in like a senseless chicken.

And watching him so, I pitied him.
He would have hated that, I knew,
as I crossed the yard, and he hastened
his pace, flashing one supercilious eye.

I expected he would run, Mr. Avoider.
Mr. Too Busy, Too Important
for a Counsel. And by the way
he dodged me, I could see he was a pro

circling around the window wells and
bushes, squeezing into corners
then raising his dark cape to chase me
back and flee again. Finally,

he spread his wings like a set
of black cards, pressed them to the grass.
He was brutal, exquisite. He held me
with one eye as I lowered the blue

basket over him, scurried back inside.
Is this it? he might have asked, peering
through the plastic slats. *After days of rising
to meet a thousand suns and cars and carrion,*

*blood against blood, is the final blow
really this soft?* Someone would come, gently
blanket him away. The house, the yard,
the skies, the jobs, dead deer, tall trees,

the wife, and, further back, the jungle gym
and big red ball and worms would all grow
small. There would be a doctor in the wings,
of course, and hope. Hope for the crow.

65 North

Because I was driving, not flying, I passed Home of the Best Gummy Bears in the World, and I entered briefly the bright theater of childhood, then returned once again to these fields, flat and frosted. Hours of this. Maybe a shack, weather-worn outbuildings, plazas for fueling and feeding, bare trees and two blank billboards so I wondered what anyone could possibly say. A windowless building set far back on tar, cut off like a prison. Because I was driving, not flying, I thought of the nameless the lonely the trapped for whom life was just more long highway. I thought of the ones who might never know even this crossing of flatlands. Who might never get out, who might never arrive at this dropping of late-day sun—inside towers and brick, rust cylinders and grids, boxcars, machinery and trucks. Who might never believe what can only be mercy—that even the grayest cement stands to glow.

Acknowledgments

Continents, even the smallest—marbles and books—take time, and *The Arrows That Choose Us*, which went through numerous incarnations and includes poems written over two decades, has its origins as far back as my childhood, at Vernon Drugs, in Worcester, Massachusetts, where I would stand in the aisle of the greeting cards, reading verse, then go home and write my own poems, confident they exceeded those on the store shelves. From there, numerous public school English teachers guided and believed in me (Mrs. Dolan, Ms. Raynor, Miss Drake and Ms. Eldridge), and I persevered "in my craft or sullen art," as Dylan Thomas put it, beyond schooling and through years of work.

I am enormously grateful to Tom Lombardo for choosing this manuscript for the 2018 Press 53 Award for Poetry and for providing the editorial guidance that brought the manuscript to this final form, and to Kevin Morgan Watson for his warmth and openness and careful attention as he designed and produced this book.

Thank you to my parents, siblings, and relatives whose love of conversation gave me a lifelong appreciation for language and stories. I am indebted to Lynn Emanuel and Ed Ochester for showing me what is possible and making me a better editor of my own poems. To friends, near and far, thank you for your sustenance over the years, for your humor and insights and honesty, and for your belief in my work; it matters more than I can say. I wish I could include all of your names. A special thank you to those who helped at key moments: Sue Abbattista, Bobbie Arganian, Michele Besant, Barbara Edelman, Cecilia Ford, Caren Harris, Terrance Hayes, Jonathan Ivry, Elena Levy-Navarro, Elizabeth Kim, Marjorie Rhine, George Savage, Sarah VilaCruz, Nancy Virtue, and Kellie Wells. Thanks to friends and colleagues at the UW-Whitewater who have nurtured and supported my writing; to my students, who continue to inspire me; and to the College of Letters and Sciences for their support. I am grateful to members of my writing group for wise counsel: Robin Chapman, Susan Elbe (in memoriam), Catherine Jagoe, Jesse Lee Kercheval, and Sara Parrell.

Finally, I hand my heart to the faithful and stalwart, to those who read one more version of a poem or manuscript over the years and remained resilient, patient, brilliant, affirming—from you I was asked just the right questions. You helped me to see my way clear. Thank you, dear ones: Joyce Dehli, Gwen Ebert, Zeki Erim, Karen Kovacik, Rick Oehling, Jeanie Tomasko, and Alison Townsend. And to Jo-Anne Lazarus, my deepest gratitude, for her courage and goodness, her constancy of love and support. Through her gentle spirit I am learning some of life's hardest lessons.

Marilyn Annucci

Marilyn Annucci's poetry and essays have appeared in numerous journals and anthologies, including *Prairie Schooner*, *Rattle*, *North American Review* and *Indiana Review*. She is the author of *Luck*, a chapbook from Parallel Press, and *Waiting Room*, winner of the 2012 Sunken Garden Poetry Prize. Originally from Worcester, Massachusetts, Marilyn worked for years as an editor and writer before earning an MFA from the University of Pittsburgh. She lives in Madison, Wisconsin, and is a professor in the Department of Languages and Literatures at the University of Wisconsin-Whitewater.

www.ingramcontent.com/pod-product-compliance
Lightning Source LLC
LaVergne TN
LVHW041344080426
835512LV00006B/606